VOICES OF MY BEING

VERSES FROM MY SOUL

SNEHA DEVASKAR

To the Universe for guiding me on my journey, to the soul that speaks
through me and to the Sneha who evolved to tell the tale

Contents

Contents

Author's Note

I never knew I could write until 19, which is when I wrote my first poem – inspired by Dilip Chitre's 'Father Returning Home'. Poems came into my life through my Guru, Vinayak Bhosale who taught me music and Ms. Preeti Shirodkar, who introduced me to the world of English Literature. Poetry came to me in phases – some days I would keep writing poems one after another and then there would be days and months, I wouldn't write anything at all.

I always thought I was meant to be a singer. I was busy practicing to be a good singer and put all my efforts in the pursuit but to no great success. On the contrary, poetry was natural, effortless. It just flowed through me and came on paper. One day, I decided to stop running behind music and see what poetry is showing to me. I learnt that she was asking me to hold her hand and show to the world what comes from the soul. And then I learnt that my music also had the same soul. They were all coming from within me and the human potential cannot be limited to one profession, one talent, one interest. Of course, one of them takes over but the others are always there. And you can choose to reveal only one of them to the world or choose to show your true self, your unlimited potential. I have now chosen to opt for the latter. For this decision, I am grateful to Happiness Coach and Spiritual Guide, Madhurima Mazumdar who is also my friend, philosopher, guide.

However, all the people mentioned above came into my life much later. It is my mother, Jyotsna Parab and my sisters who've raised me and made me capable enough to venture out into the world. They did whatever was in their best capacity to make me the person that I am today. I would like to extend gratitude to my family, friends and all the people whom I met in life – the ones who are around and the ones who moved on – for they contributed to my journey as a person and those experiences revealed themselves through my poems. I am grateful to my son, Anaahat, for he gave me a different identity, purpose, and perspective.

I want to extend my deepest gratitude to my friends Kirti Chaturvedi, Sangita Marda Agarwal, Sanya Khurana and the Notion Press team who helped me in this process of publishing my collection – a dream I kept to myself for the longest of time. I also want to thank Aarti Nadekar and Mugdha Nene for the beautiful artwork they've added to my book. Although the poems have an inherent imagery, they have given my poems a concrete, visual form. I was also able to create a few of these illustrations which were later brought to the digital form by Aarti. Credit for uncovering this version of me goes to Piyuesh Modi, my sketchnotes trainer and dear friend, Sayli Ghanekar Potdar who made me believe that

I could draw and paint some day. I am immensely grateful to Vikas Khot for his guidance and Renuka Khot for shooting my portrait and making me look like an author of another league.

Lastly, I thank the Universe for choosing me and helping me see the fulfilment of my dream and supporting me throughout.

With limitless gratitude,
Sneha
September 2023

Of Love, Hope and Desire

MAN

She wants a heart
That beats for her and with her,
Hands that give her weak hands
The strength to break the shackles of fate.
She needs feet on which
She could stand and feel rock solid
She needs a reassurance
That her faith will surpass all odds.
She needs a man
Whom she could call her 'Man',
Or at least 'A man'.

MUSE

Make me not your Muse,
Who stands like a portrait in your poems,
Lifeless and public.
Make me the energy of your poem.
Let me flow through your thoughts.
Let me be omnipresent in your work,
That can't be seen,
But is there.
Let me breathe through your creativity,
A constant process which when stops
Takes life out of a thing.
Don't make me your pen;
Let me be the ink that writes,
The one that leaves an imprint,
That fills in an urge to be traced.

Immortalize this tiny sprite
As a gift for
Loving you deeply.

GIRL AT THE STATION

She stands there,
At the threshold
Anxious to take the plunge;
Timid to face the world,
Yet determined to stand.
She is dreamy,
Lost in thoughts,
Aspiring company,
Wishing someone would come from behind
Hug her and kiss on her shoulders;
Just as tiny droplets of rain, each one,
Place a peck on her cheeks
As if they were messages filled with passion
Sent by a distant lover
Who wishes to cross the seas for her.

WAITING FOR YOU

When these long hours traverse the night
To touch the bright, colourful dawn,
I keep mumbling inside my mind,
Of how much I love you
And how much I pine for you.

I feel the pain of longing,
As if I were walking on a lonely road
Without a shadow by my side.
I feel the bruise of distance
That time marks between us
When you are gone.

And then, I keep waiting
For your handsome face
To bestow a kiss on my cheek,
To assure me you are by my side
And I am under your spell.

DESIRE

His towering body upon mine,
Like the cool shadow
Amid scorching heat.
His warm embrace entrapping me
Like comfort getting cosy.
His eyes overflowing with love,
Like oasis in a desert.
His touch, traversing my body,
Like Midas turning me into gold.
His kiss on my moist lips
Like lovers under Mistletoe.
His thirst for my nape,
Like plucking a flower to drink its dew.
His body across mine
Like two pieces striving to be one.

If this is love,
This is beautiful,
This is peaceful,
This is euphoric,
This is soothing,
This is balmy,
This is desire.

LOVE

Your eyes met mine,
And mine yours.
This time, differently,
This time, we were locked,
You inside me,
I inside you;
Experiencing a moment of euphoria.
I, elated, and you, too.
But not a word or two,
Or even the slightest remark.
Nothing changed, except the insides.
They experienced a moment of ecstasy,
Few seconds which meant eternity,
To you, and yes, to me, too.

No carnal desires involved,
But a gaze touched my soul,
Perhaps no intimacy involved,
But yes, I saw a man after all.
I saw a man,
Who looked straight into a woman's eyes,
And that showed me,
Twinkling stars in broad daylight.
Is this what 'Love' feels like?

ETERNITY

Walking with you on these lonely streets
In the green bushes,
I always realised while holding your hands,
This is the idyllic existence
That I always yearned for.
Every moment with you
Felt like eternity.

Yet, when I came home,
I realised,
Eternity is a creation of the mind;
It ends where you want it to —
where you start thinking of your existence.
and in a moment, everything is swapped.

The heat of your body,
That gives me tranquillity is far away.
I am left cold, aloof,
Far away from you.
Yearning for you.
Indulging in nostalgia.

SOLACE

In your warm embrace,
I find solace.
When you look deep into my eyes,
It feels like someone is swimming down my soul
Clearing the bed of weeds;
Making the fish dance to the rhythm of my ocean –
Beautiful fish, multi-coloured, full of life.

When your thirsty lips kiss mine
It feels like someone is
Pouring a pitcher-full of 'Amrit' into me;
Giving me the boon of longevity.

When your hands move past my body,
Traversing known routes,
It feels like
In flesh and bone, we are one.
In soul, we are one.
In love, we are one.

WHO ARE YOU?

You are neither my past,
Nor present nor future.
You are my now —
This moment, this millisecond
Of life, of breathlessness,
Of catching up on that lost breath,
And regaining composure.

You are my victory.
My anticipation of a
Bigger, fuller life,
Of a softer touch,
Of a pleasant surprise,
Of a hard-to-believe but
Yes-it's-happening.

You are my promise to myself,
To live regal,
To dance pagan,
To sing like a nightingale,
And exit with a swan song.

DEAR SOULMATE

My soul wanders in search of some calm,
Roams around aimlessly.
At times walks along set paths,
At times drifts across,
Enters a dark, unknown tunnel,
To find light at the end.
But to no response.
My soul wanders like a barking dog,
Eyeing each door, each turn,
With expectations,
Barking so that someone would listen.
But loses hope like a puppy does.
My soul flies high like an eagle in the noon
With no respite,
Bald in the heat,
Observing from higher and higher,
Only to find distance increasing.

My soul finds peace
When it comes to your shade.
That is where my pangs find an end.
It is a heavenly feeling —
Deeper than the dark of the night,
Cooler than the face of the moon,
Warmer than the kiss of a love,
Peaceful and peaceful.

ONE FINE DAY

And one fine day,
I realized, I can't take it anymore.
I've had enough of you;
Your priorities, your demands,
Your dislikes, your interests,
Your schedules, your this, your that.

So one fine day,
I decided, I won't take it anymore.
I've had enough of you
And now I want myself back.
So I went down memory lane,
To locate myself
But was taken by surprise.

There was neither me,
Nor my shadow,
Not even my reflection!
Only you were peeping
Through my eyes,
And you were gleaming
Through my skin,
And you were dictating
My desires.

And that fine day,
I realized, I am incomplete without you.
My life isn't mine,
If you aren't a part of it.
My beauty isn't beauty,
If you don't adore it.
My love isn't love,
If you don't reciprocate.

So that fine day,
I realized,
My love for you exceeds,
My ego, my pain, my being.
'Coz your love for me exceeds,
Our egos, our discord, our being

THE MAN

Sparkling, naughty eyes
And that arrogant smile,
Delicate, long fingers
And that determined gait.
He is not really my kind
But so much mine.
He is the ruthless warrior,
But a gentle king.
He is the trust
That steadfastness does really exist,
That every promise made
Shall be fulfilled,
That every soft touch
Shall be pure,
That every moment of love
Shall be divine,
That every difficult moment
Shall be dealt with a spine,
That every breath taken
Shall breathe life into mine.

FOR THAT ONE MOMENT

For that one moment,
When I want you to be mine,
Will you surrender?
For that one moment,
When I want you to read my eyes,
Will you dive into them?
For that one moment,
When I want you to pacify me,
Will you touch my soul?
For that one moment,
When I want to be a part of you,
Will you bring time to a standstill?

IF I COULD...

If I could,
I would never let you go,
Part ways or leave me for a second.
I would make you sit beside me all the time,
And talk to me and listen to me,
And snuggle beside me all the time.

If I could,
I would make you realize,
What happens to me
When you leave me on my own.
When you leave me on my own,
A part of me detaches
And the whole of me goes defunct.

If I could,
I would make time seem immaterial
Only let love conquer all;
And let love live between us,
For now, and for ever.

If I could,
I would never let death come between us.
I would die the very moment
You decide to end it all.
'Coz for me,
Being with you is the
End All and Be All.
No moment before you,
No moment after you,
No moment without you.

MAKE LOVE

Glistening with sensuality,
You lie there tired,
Frozen, in deep slumber...

Your bare back says otherwise.
It wants me to crash on you,
To turn you around,
And suck the two mounds,
That overflow with femininity,
While I am eyeing
Your curvaceous bottom,
That has in store
Several heaps of unexplored passion.
Your tresses,
Falling on your nape,
Like flowers during blossom time,
Tempt me to play with them,
Pull them, love them,
Lie under their shade,
Like a traveller under a tree;
While your juicy, fleshy fingers
Look like they must be devoured.

Oh! How I wish to wake you up
And make love to you,
Awaken your senses,
And bathe in carnal pleasure,
Like a dying, old soul,
That wishes to live one last time.

Of Motherhood

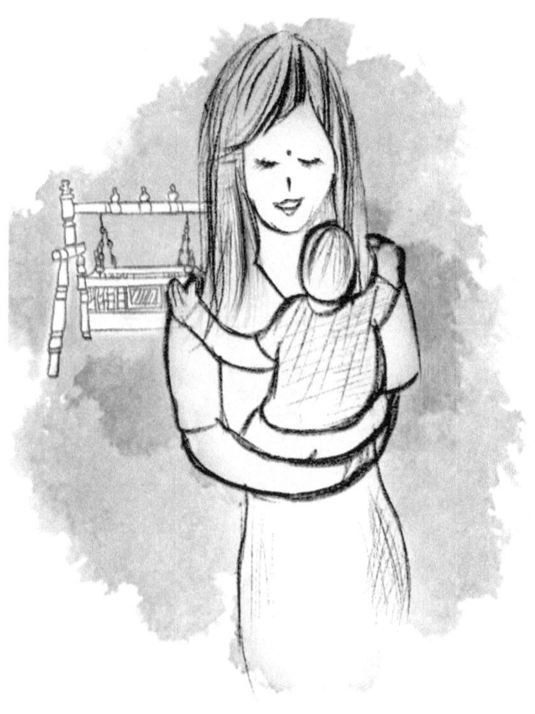

GIFTS OF MOTHERHOOD

As you hold me close to you,
In deep sleep,
Your little tummy nudges mine
As you breathe in, breathe out
Oblivious to the running of the world,
I realize the gifts of proximity.
As you look for me at the end of the day,
And wrap your little arms around my waist upon seeing me,
I realize the joys of affection.
I realize my body doesn't make a difference to you,
Its softness is cushion to you
And the hug is a reassurance.
As you cheer me when I score well in my tests,
Get promoted at work,
Get excited about my performance
And ask me questions to satiate your curious self
I realize, I matter.
As you keep coming back to me,
Consistently, unconditionally,
Planting kisses on my cheeks out of nowhere
I realize the gifts of motherhood.

AAI

He squeezes me in hugs
And smothers me with kisses
His eyes start sparkling
When he sees me around

His love is unconditional
My presence is enough for him
He taught me how to love me
Without any inhibition

He disagrees and disapproves
But loves me nonetheless
He is more my present of love
Than a future of inheritance

He shows some of my traits
And some are just not mine
He chose me to be his mother
And that's just enough & fine

I love him like no other
And that's the best of me
I strive to be a better human
For him, I'm the most suitable Aai[1]

Of Sadness, Agony & Pain…

DETACHMENT

The home stands homeless
The body is no more yours.
When you look into the mirror
It refuses your identity.

The clothes say, 'You are not worth them'.
You wear something that 'allows' you to.
Finally, you leave your historied paradise.

The loner in you travels through crowded trains
You look here and there but no one seems to care.
You reach the place you want to
But no one wants you to share.

You come out of the place.
You find lots of light around,
But none of it wants to seep into you
None of it wants to enlighten you

You went as a loner,
You came back as the same.
The streetlights still barking at you,
But now, you don't care.

The homeless home awaits you,
It understands, you still, are attached.
When the night falls, you enter the cottage of the mind.
It asks you, "Where had you been?"
You start pondering,
Did I forget my 'Self' somewhere?

WHAT WENT WRONG

Endless nights proceed,
With weepy eyes,
Moist pillows,
And a lonely heart
Trying to figure out
What went wrong.

She waits, like her mother
For her child to sleep,
So that he does not witness
Her mute cries,
Her bleeding wounds,
Her butchered heart.

Night passes like
A decelerated train journey
To a destination she has no intention to reach,
Just waiting for stations to pass
Her eyes close for some seconds
And she wakes up at every jerk
As if the train reminds her,
She is not supposed to sleep.

She wakes up to
Tired mornings
Finishes her chores like a robot
But the battery discharges
Within an hour or two.

She drags her body to work,
As if it were several logs of wood.
Here, she is a different person.
Cracking jokes all the time,
Laughing at herself,
As if she cut ties with
Her personal life.

As the clock says, "Evening",
She rushes to the door,
Leaves the place,
Picks her child,
Finishes the chores,
Feeds her baby,
Like an expert mom.

Her life works in tandem
With her plan.
Meticulously designed
To ensure her child
Never has to answer,
"What went wrong?"

As the night approaches,
Fear engulfs her.
She fears the coming of the night.
Her mind throws the question
Like a brick on her forehead,
"What went wrong?"

She ponders over it,
And sleeps only when
Her eyes are tired of
Keeping awake.

STRANGER THINGS

It's weird to estrange yourself
From a person you once loved;
To engage in small talk
And ask permissions for the smallest of favours
Lest they become another reason for a tiff.

You know what's funny?
You know this stranger too well
To know how and what and when
Yet you choose to drift apart
For the sake of your sanity and theirs.

You know what's bad?
That you go through the suffering
Conscious of the turmoil
Putting extra effort into 'not giving'
To compensate for the 'over giving'

You know what's worse?
You carry the burden of the scars
Into the dynamics with a stranger
You want to now call your own.

Strangers are best when they are strangers
If they have a past with you,
You mess it up for them
And the rest that follow.
What's even worse,
You mess it most for yourself.

DARKNESS

I wait for the night to engulf me.
As darkness unfurls,
I feel home,
I feel like I'm in a womb.

Even the slightest flicker
Of light puts me to unrest.
I fidget like a paranoid
To shut the door
And shut myself in.

Once in the darkness
Of my creation,
I feel anonymous
And that's so balmy.

Anonymous
Is anyone and everyone.
Anonymity –
Wipe your identity
And be what you want
Or don't be anything at all.
You are neither big nor small.
You are you,

Or perhaps, not even you.
You cannot see yourself
You can just hear
The sounds of your inner self
That have been roaring since
A long time now
But you couldn't pay attention
'Coz your attention was devoted
To the chaos of the world.

Now listen to your self
Or any self
Because you are anonymous
What you say is not
What "you" have said.
It is an anonymous dialogue
Between your inner self
And the anonymous speaker
That resides inside you.

Don't worry.
Anonymity has a trump card called
"No judgment/No opinion/
No sentence/No punishment"
Just a kind demeanor
To accept what you say
And how you say.

Darkness is cozy,
Darkness is blind,
Darkness is beautiful,
Darkness is kind.

BROKEN VASE

Broken but beautiful,
Beautiful but broken,
The vase is standing still,
Weeping, singing melancholic tunes,
Calling out to its restorer,
Waiting for him to restore its lost stature.

He comes to the room,
Lights up the dark,
And turns to the table,
Where the vase stands,
Cold, dejected, motionless.

His warm hands
Touch the vase,
And a tiny piece chips off,
As if the vase had been
Holding on its tears for long.
As if the vase breaks down,
In his warm embrace.

He fixes the cracks
And heals the bruises.
He puts together the broken pieces

And mends the vase.
With love and care,
He paints the vase anew,
As if bringing it to life again,
Bringing it out of the dead.

He knows the cracks are
No more visible to the naked eye.
But the insides still have the scars.
He resurrects the vase day in day out,
By holding it between his affectionate palms.
He is a potter,
Designing new vases,
But this broken vase,
Is his dearest possession.
Its beauty resides in his eyes,
Its strength resides in his warmth.

UNFAIR!

Tossing and turning
In my warm, cosy bed,
I keep thinking of her.
Must she be asleep?
Sound asleep?
Must she be seeing flashes of those moments
When she was wronged?
Shoved out like a particle of dust?
Thrown on the roads like litter?

How much angst must she be living with?
Under that sweet face, that innocent smile,
Must she be holding a terrible urge
To set this world on fire?
To destroy it in a flash of a second?
To fix the unfairness she has been
Experiencing all this while?

"What do I want now?",
Asks my mind.
I want to go to her
Sleep beside her
Take her in my warm embrace
And wipe out all the angst

She keeps inside her bosom.
I want to milk out
All the love I have inside mine
And nourish her existence.
I want her to bloom into
The most beautiful flower,
With no thorns,
And a fragrance so sweet
That makes you forget
all the woes of the world.

ANCHORLESS

Anchorless, here I stand
Waiting for a lighthouse
To show me the way.

The scorching sun,
The balmy moon,
The cool blue sea,
Are all here,
Yet there is no direction to my way.
I envy the flight of the birds
And the swims of the sea beings.

Here I am,
Chained, motionless, stuck
Like a prisoner of the sea
That mocks at my tininess
Before its blue expanse.
The stillness of its waters,
Its salty nature,
Only serve to heighten my pain,
Increase my thirst.
But I am here to learn my lesson,
From the waters,
That reflect the sunshine,

That let droplets of diamonds
Float on the surface
And shine like stars,
Through day, through night.

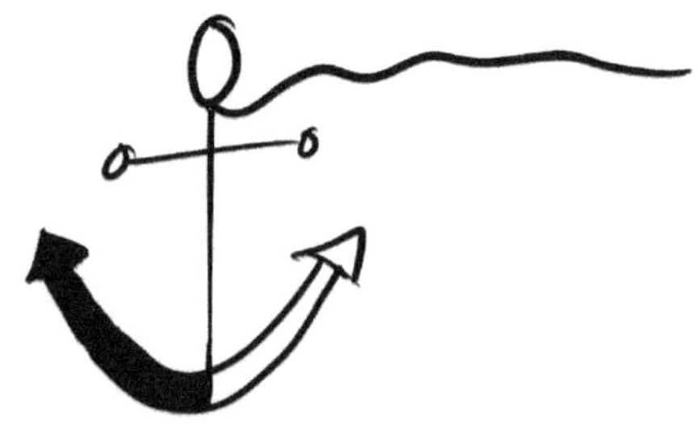

THE DEMONS

As I sleep burying my head into these pillows
You have no idea what demons dance over my head
You see my bare back and you find it sultry
You say I am yours, not caring once
How they poke me with their needle hooks
I bear it all because I have to be with you.
I lie to you of how happy I am
In your company.
You are just an escape
From their constant poking.
I hug you and enter your sacred space.
I feel grounded
'Coz I am cut off from the trauma world
For the time I am in your warm embrace.

As I step out again, they catch hold of me
I start bleeding inside but I can't tell you.
You won't believe me.
So I smile back at you
And pretend to be happy
While inside me, I am crumbling.
And I fail at telling you what hurts me
'Coz I am scared to
Break the sanctity of the moment.

I am neither here nor there,
Neither with you nor myself,
Neither happy nor elated.
I am just struggling to hold myself together
While the demons of my mind
Keep poking me inch by inch
Biting me and nibbling me
And sucking the blood out of me.

HALF THOUGHTS

Half thoughts,
Dark nightmares...
The fingers itch to write something
But the brain switches off mid-way.
That which has to come out in
Black and white
Never propels out of the mind.

Hanging from the ceiling,
I look at the world below.
The world hasn't changed,
People are breathing
Just as they were.
Birds are chirping like they always did,
Welcoming the early monsoon.
Mrudgandhaa.
Yes, that's my name.
Where's she?
Can someone smell her? Mrudgandhaa?
Or is she lost in this concrete jungle?
Hunted down like a prey?
She is running for her life,
Tired yet running,
Facing the wrath of everyone;

As if she stole a piece from each one,
And is now flaunting it as her own.
No, she didn't.
She is already endowed.
She has been misread.
And she wants to tell that to all.
But the spears,
They are all coming towards her.
She has two choices.
Kill herself or get killed.
In any case,
Her life would cease to exist.
And that looks like the answer to all.

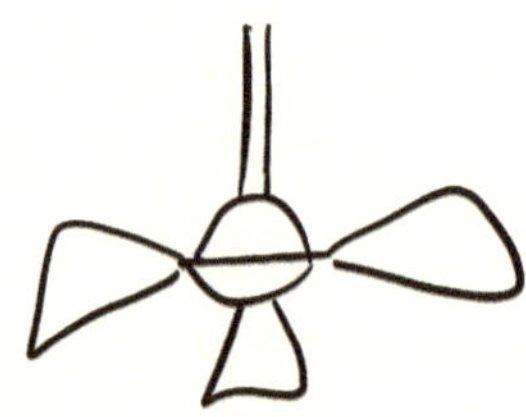

Of Survival, Triumphs and Revival

STAND TALL.

Running away isn't the option darling,
Weeping your heart out also isn't.
The only way out is through.
Go through it, deal with it,
Face it with a face tall.
Stand before the storm
Like the calm before the storm.
Let it pass; let it break you.
But you stand there like
An ancient tree with dark, dense roots.
The leaves may sway,
The flowers may wither;
The roots will stay.
Clench them for a moment
And let loose the next.
They will stand their ground
And hold you in place.
The storm will subside
And the sun will shine.
Leaves will grow
And flowers will bloom
And fruits will bear.

This too shall pass.
Remember:
This too shall pass.

ALONE

At the end of it all,
You're still going to be alone.
No matter how many people surround you,
How much they say, they love you
The fact is that at the end of it all,
It's only going to be you.

Why wait till the end?
It is here, right here,
In this moment!
Take a breath
And you'd realize the whole game is yours
You're the loser.
But if you think of it,
You can also be the sole winner.

They'd teach you, man is a social animal
And you need to let society mark your territory;
But that's just their way of expanding their territory
And barging into yours.

Hold, my girl.
Take control of your life.
If you were born alone
And you'll die alone,
Why then do you want another?

Companionship is good,
But alone is awesome,
If you teach yourself,
Alone is awesome,
Alone would indeed be awesome.

Take this chance,
C'mon, take charge.
Sometimes you gotta swim,
Sometimes you gotta fly,
Sometimes you just gotta stand on your two feet
And just breathe.

LIFE IS A TOAST, BABY!

I wish someday,
You hear the cries
That scream beyond drumrolls;
You read not just the lines
But realize the meaning that they convey;
You understand the silence,
Not misinterpret it as anger;
You take a step forward
To give that what is wanted;
You fumble once or twice
But make an effort to dance.
'Coz life is a toast
You need to raise it
Before you take a sip.

PHOENIX

She will rise like a phoenix,
Trust me, she will soar.
Though she was burnt to ashes,
She will smear the same ashes
Across her body,
And live like a Yogini.
She will be above all –
Fear, anger, hatred, insecurity,
Everything that pulls her back.
She will fly against the winds,
And swim across the waves.
All she needs right now
Is your hand to clutch on to,
Your love to heal her parched soul,
Your light to illuminate her existence,
And you will notice her rise;
Rise like never before.
Trust me, she will soar.

Other Poems

MODERN DAY

Smoke shoots from the factories,

From the trash,

From the grass.

A dim sunlight unveils itself

At the planned hour, reluctantly.

Ants crawl out of their forts

To earn material ends.

One looks like the other,

The other like another.

Each one crawling in and out

And up and down

And back and forth,

Like a corpse.

They settle before machines,

To work like machines,

To undo the feat of their forerunners.

Not realizing,

When it is day

And when it is not.

When the clock summons

The planned hour,

They go back to their anthills,

Tired, melancholic, sleepy.

They crawl into their beds,

And die for a few hours.
And the world dies with them.

The next morning comes,
Awakens them at the planned hour,
To pull the same burden for the next day.

ETHERISED UPON A TABLE

She lies on the bed,
Like a patient etherised upon a table.
She bears his kisses
Like a bitter tablet,
His body upon her
Like a bedding provided by the nurse,
His hands on her arms
Like a drip
His nails as syringes.
She gives him pleasure.
He fills her treasure.
When an hour passes away,
The head of the brothel coughs at the door;
He leaves her there,
Just as she was —
A pious nun
Waiting for the next customer to enter.

LAJJA

You hypocrites,
I am talking to you.

You, who tell her what to wear,
What not to wear,
How to step out
And when to go home.

You, who keep ogling at her,
On the streets, in the mall,
On the screen, on the stops

You, who letch at her,
Waiting for the moment
Her pallu slips,
Her shirt unbuttons,
Her jeans reveals the line.

You, who tell her,
Not to hug,
Not to kiss,
No, no, not in public.

You, who make it hard for her to exist,
You, who make her deny her sexuality,
You, who make it hard for her to trust
Her body, her instincts, her love.

And what do you call it?
Lajja, Sharam, Pardah, Izzat!
So it is important for you
That the woman inside her dies each day
Trying to keep it intact;
Burning her desires,
Suppressing her emotions,
Living for the sake of death

What do you make her at the end?
Another hypocrite who wants one thing
And asks for another.

You hypocrites,
What do you know about Lajja?
Do you know what it means?
Why was it created?

It was created for her,
To coil herself in when she felt unsafe,
And to put a farce when
When she wished to tease him,
And uncoil herself in his embrace,
When she wanted to have it.

You hypocrites,
You can never understand,
Because all this human
And you are beasts.

BEYOND THE FACE

Set loose the passion dumped inside your hair,
O, daughter of the new moon.
Show twinkling stars in broad daylight
To the needful,
Blink your eyes, O lady,
And bless the world with a hurricane,
Stretch your lips a bit
And kill the world with your beauty.
Let them get up with a start
And stare at you.

Don't worry!
You won't lose your virtue
'Coz you have set your boundaries.
You know you are chaste.
Tempt the world around
So that their sins overpower,
And they are drowned,
And penalized for what they did to you.

Don't worship yourself,
Worship your virtue,
And you will find people around you
Who worship you and your virtue.
And show to the world how
Beauty lies beyond the face.

UNFATHOMABLE

Why is life so complicated?
Or is it we who make it complicated?
What do we get out of thinking so much?
Why aren't we potent enough
To understand our own minds?
Is this impotence a part of life?
Or is it a part of feeling things
And then finding out
That some things are just unfathomable?

Questions unanswered
Always make me restless.
I am a believer of the justness of things
And when life acts in an
Unjustified manner,
I am hell bent on finding its reasons.
I end up not getting any
And then I am forced to think on the same lines.

Why is life so complicated?
Or is it we who make it complicated?
What do we get out of thinking so much?
Why aren't we potent enough
To understand our own minds?

ADDRESSED TO MY POETRY

You are my daughter,
My reflection,
Outrageous, outspoken,
Direct, out in the open.
All set to challenge
The word of the world.

When I had heard of
Parvati creating Gunesha
Out of her sweat,
I had dismissed it
Assuming it to be myth.

Now, I realize,
It wasn't.
He was all that she had,
All that she had created of her own.
He was her priciest possession.
So when he steadfastly guarded her,
She felt pride.
When he was beheaded,
She cried.
And when resurrected,

She was filled with joy;
When made the first to be revered,
She felt elated;
And when made the Lord of the Arts,
Science, Wisdom and Intellect,
She rejoiced,
Because he was her creation.

Aren't you the same to me?
Don't you subject me to labour
When you have to come out in the open?
Aren't you the one
Created by my sweat, turmoil,
Distress and joy?

Such a fool I had been
All this long,
For wanting a daughter;
When you are here,
By my side, at all times —
Holding me,
Consoling me,
And lashing out at people,
When I am at a loss of words.
As if you are here
To get back at the world;
For stabbing so many of my daughters,
Sisters and mothers
Who cannot see the light of the day.

Let me tell you
My dear daughter,
Your purpose is this —
To speak for the mute,
To listen for the deaf,
To uplift the broken heart,
To cheer the depressed soul,
To fix all that is wrong.

PORTRAIT OF A POET

Inside the frame
Of a human body,
Resides a heart
That is home to
A myriad emotions.

Love and pain are
Permanent tenants
Just like night and day
In life.

This heart, they say,
Weeps when need be,
And writes when tears
Are left to dry.

This heart, it seems,
Knows the route to many others,
Understands their woes,
And pens their sorrow.

This heart, they believe,
Is an ordinary one.
But they don't realize,
It can heal the parched soul.

This heart, he says,
Is connected to the ultimate Soul,
That which leaves one form for another,
To read the life of mankind.

Reference

[1] Aai stands for Mother in Marathi